Activities for 3-5 year olds

Food

 Brilliant Publications

Adrienne Walton

We hope you enjoy using this book. If you would like further information on other titles published by Brilliant Publications, please write to the address given below.

Note: to avoid the clumsy 'he/she', the child is referred to throughout as 'he'.

Published by Brilliant Publications, The Old School Yard, Leighton Road, Northall, Dunstable, Bedfordshire LU6 2HA

Written by Adrienne Walton
Illustrated by Frank Endersby

Printed in Malta by Interprint Limited

© Adrienne Walton
ISBN 1 897675 57 7

First published 1999
10 9 8 7 6 5 4 3 2 1

Contents

Introduction

Talking about, handling, preparing and eating food have instant appeal for young children and offer an excellent starting point from which to explore a whole variety of learning experiences.

The activities in this book are organized to work within the framework of the QCA's Desirable Learning Outcomes and take into account children's developing intellectual, social and physical skills focusing, upon ideas that will encourage the growth of a positive self-image and a positive attitude to others.

Many of the activities provide opportunities to teach children about the importance of hygiene in food preparation and how to use kitchen tools and equipment safely. Other activities help to promote healthy eating habits and may encourage children to be more adventurous in trying different foods.

All the activities are based on the principle that young children learn best by 'doing', so wherever possible children should be encouraged to do as much as they can for themselves and be supervised to handle real objects and use real tools. Giving children ample opportunities to talk about what they are doing is also a vitally important part of the learning process.

Above all, learning should be enjoyable, so try to adopt a play approach as much as possible and be prepared to be flexible to meet the children's individual needs and accommodate their interests.

This book uses materials that are likely to be readily available within your class or group, or that can be gathered from the children's families or carers.

Cafe

What children should learn

Language and literacy – to develop speaking and listening skills in a group whilst planning a new role-play area.

What you need

A quiet place to talk; a large sheet of paper and a marker pen to record ideas.

Activity

Sit the children comfortably in a circle on the floor so that everyone feels able to contribute. Ask: 'What is a cafe? Who can tell me what happens there?' Ask the children to share their own experiences of eating out'. Ask, 'Who works in a cafe?' and 'What food might they serve?' Lead the children to think about what equipment they may need to collect, in order to set up their own cafe. List the children's ideas on the large sheet of paper, recording each child's name next to their contributions. Encourage the children to bring things from home for the new cafe, such as cut-out pictures of food, or a menu from McDonald's.

Extension

Act out different role-plays; an adult playing alongside the children could demonstrate the differing tasks of the waiter/waitress, cook or customer. A visit from a real cook or waiter to talk about their job could enhance the children's learning.

Talk about

Once the children have had the opportunity to use the cafe, you could hold further discussions on how to use new pieces of equipment, such as a notepad to write down orders or a whisk for beating eggs.

Make a menu for the cafe

What children should learn

Language and literacy – to know that words and pictures carry meaning; to develop an awareness of the different purposes of writing.

What you need

A selection of menus from cafes and restaurants; paper, pencils, crayons and pens; alphabet and number lines to provide a model for the children's writing; plastic or salt dough food; food pictures cut from magazines to provide models for the children's drawings.

Activity

Display the menus and discuss with the children the information contained, together with the layout of the types of food, ie starters, main course, desserts, beverages. Discuss the types of food to be included on your menu and what format it should take – booklet or single sheet, for example. Ask each child to choose a dish or type of food and to draw it, then to write a description for it. Cut them out and glue them on the group menu.

Extension

Use your new menu in the cafe to extend the role-play. Use a chalkboard or easel to write down 'Today's Specials', and with the children's help create a new list. Introduce notepads for the waiters to write down the food orders and squared or lined paper for the children to write down the customers' bills and receipts. Make 'Open' and 'Closed' signs.

Talk about

Talk about the different sorts of writing the children have produced for the cafe. The orders or bills could be displayed with labels to identify each child's work. Encourage the children to help you read back their work, praising their achievements.

Yum and yuk!

What children should learn

Language and literacy – to speak and listen in a group, expressing likes and dislikes; to record their ideas.

What you need

Paper plates or paper cut into large circles; paper cut into speech bubble shapes; collage materials, eg fabric scraps, gummed paper, tissue paper, shiny paper, bottle tops, buttons, corks; coloured felt-tipped pens.

Activity

In a small group, start the discussion by talking about your own food likes and dislikes. For example 'I really like strawberries – *yum!*', 'I don't like beetroot – *yuk!*' Encourage the children to talk about their food likes and dislikes and to take it in turns to share these with other group members. Next, help each child to select materials to make a collage picture of his face. Ask them to repeat what they like and dislike so that you can write down their words on a speech bubble for other people to read. Display the collage faces and speech bubbles together, preferably at child height. Help each child to read his writing back to you.

Extension

Introduce a 'food tasting' session where you all try more unusual foods, like mango or avocado. Record on a chart the 'yums' and 'yuks' for each child's reaction to the different foods tasted.

Talk about

Talk about sweet and savoury foods – see if the children can sort foods into these categories. Talk about what happens if you eat too many sweet foods and the importance of trying to eat a balanced diet.

A food alphabet

What children should learn

Language and literacy – to associate letter shapes with letter sounds and objects and to begin to write letter shapes.

What you need

An alphabet chart; plastic letter shapes; a large sheet of paper and an easel; thick felt-tipped pens; a selection of food items that match the letter of the alphabet you are using, for example for 'b': banana, baked beans, bread; a drawstring bag.

Activity

Before the children arrive, place the food items in the drawstring bag. Display your chosen letter and the alphabet chart on the easel. Sit the children around you and discuss the shape and sound of the letter displayed. Ask them to practise writing it in the air, describing the way to write it. Ask one child to pick an item from the bag and discuss the link between the item and the letter, writing on the chart the letter and the name of the object. Discuss and make a list of the remaining objects that are in the bag.

Extension

Read *Eating the Alphabet – Fruits and Vegetables from A to Z* by Lois Ehlert and make your own 'food alphabet' frieze with all the children contributing pictures and writing.

Talk about

Play a guessing game by encouraging the children to ask questions about the food items hidden in the bag, such as 'Is it red?', 'Is it sweet?', 'Is it a vegetable?', 'Do you have to cook it?' Encourage the children to take it in turns to ask and answer the questions.

The shopping game

What children should learn

Language and literacy – to develop visual and auditory memory skills; gain confidence at speaking in a group.

What you need

A shopping basket; a selection of food items; a cloth to cover the basket.

Activity

Place the items of food on the table. Sit the children in a circle around the basket. The first child starts the game by choosing an item from the table and placing it in the basket. Whilst she does this, say, 'Hannah went shopping and she bought a *loaf of bread.'* Encourage all the children to repeat it with you and place the cloth over the basket. Ask a second child to choose an item and then place it in the covered basket, whilst you say: 'Hannah went shopping and she bought a *loaf of bread.* Jamie went shopping and he bought a *jar of honey.'* Work around the circle until everyone has had a turn, encouraging the children to join in with each statement.

Extension

To help the children recall and to learn about letter sounds, encourage each child to choose a food item that starts with the same letter as their name, for example Ben buys bananas, Polly buys pasta. This could be extended further by the children taking turns in alphabetical order, so that Alice goes first followed by Ben, followed by Danielle, followed by Hassan and so on.

Talk about

Encourage the children to talk about their real shopping experiences. Where does their family go to get the shopping? Who chooses what goes in the basket or trolley? How do they pay for their shopping?

The Very Hungry Caterpillar

What children should learn

Language and literacy – to enjoy sharing books and making up their own stories.

What you need

A copy of *The Very Hungry Caterpillar* by Eric Carle; a large felt-covered board; felt scraps and fabric in assorted colours; Velcro or Blu-tac.

Activity

Using the felt, cut the following shapes: a moon, a sun, a caterpillar, a leaf, one apple, two pears, three plums, four strawberries, five oranges, a butterfly. Fix Velcro or Blu-tac to the back of them so that they can be attached to the storyboard and moved around. Sit the children in a group. Read the story, showing them the pictures in the book and pointing to the writing. Tell the story again, leaving gaps as you read, helping the children take turns to find the characters or objects in the story. As they learn the story, the children will join in without being prompted by an adult.

Extension

Encourage the children to make some of the other foods that the caterpillar eats, to use on the storyboard. These could be drawn first of all on paper and then made from felt and fabric.

Talk about

Encourage the children to adapt the original and make up their own stories by substituting different creatures for the caterpillar and using their own favourite foods. Help them to use storytelling language when telling their stories and support them in thinking of alternative endings.

Sorting Smarties

What children should learn

Mathematics – to develop sorting, matching and counting skills; to begin to understand the concept of more and less.

What you need

A tube of Smarties; a large plate or sorting tray.

Activity

Tip out the Smarties onto a large plate or sorting tray and encourage the children to sort them by colour into groups. Ask questions such as 'How many blue Smarties did you find?', 'How many green ones?', 'Do you think there are more blue Smarties or more green Smarties?' Encourage the children to arrange the two groups of Smarties into lines side by side so that they can make a direct comparison. Encourage the children to count the number of Smarties in each line and to point to each Smartie as they count, offering support where necessary. Ask each child to repeat this process, choosing two different colours of Smarties until all the colours have been counted and compared.

Extension

Can the children place the groups of Smarties in numerical order? Does each Smartie tube contain the same quantity of each colour?

Talk about

Use the language of comparison: more/less than, bigger/smaller number than, biggest/smallest group, most/least and encourage the children to use this language too.

Teddy bears' breakfast

What children should learn

Mathematics – to sort by size; to use mathematical language to describe different sizes.

What you need

Three teddy bears of different sizes to represent Daddy, Mummy and Baby Bear; one of each of the following in large, medium and small sizes: plates, bowls, cups, saucers and spoons.

Activity

The day before you carry out the activity, tell the children the story of 'Goldilocks and the Three Bears'. Introduce the three teddies to the children as the three bears. Tell them that the bears have a problem with which they need some help to sort out. Say something like, 'When the washing up was done, all the cups, saucers, plates, bowls and spoons got muddled up and now the bears want to get things ready for their breakfast, so can we help to sort things out?' Ask different children in turn if they can sort out first the plates, then the bowls, then the cups, the saucers and the spoons.

Extension

Using wooden building blocks, can the children make three beds of different sizes for the three bears? Using strips of card and scraps of coloured paper and material to decorate, can the children make three hats of different sizes to fit the three bears?

Talk about

As the children sort out the bears' crockery, talk to them about the different sizes and make comparisons. Discuss what the children eat for breakfast and what crockery they use.

Favourite fruit survey

What children should learn

Mathematics – to collect, organize and interpret data.

What you need

An apple, an orange and a banana; green, orange and yellow sticky labels; a list of everyone's name in the group, attached to a clipboard.

Activity

Tell the children that you want to go shopping to buy some fruit for everyone to share, but you would like to find out which fruit (apple, orange or banana) each child prefers so that you know how many of each type to buy. The children should work in pairs to carry out their survey. Explain that they will need to ask everyone in turn, which fruit they like best? and ask each child to find the corresponding sticker and stick it next to their name on the list.

Extension

Ask the children to count the different coloured stickers to find out how many children liked each fruit. Can they tell you which fruit was the favourite? Which fruit was the least popular? Help the children to display the information in a block graph to make it easier to count and make comparisons.

Talk about

Was there anyone in the group who didn't like any of the fruits? How was that infomation shown on the group list or graph? Can the children make up their own survey questions to ask other members of the group?

Biscuit tin

What children should learn

Mathematics – to recognize, name and describe common shapes.

What you need

A large tin of assorted biscuits; plates to sort the biscuits on to; children with clean hands.

Activity

Ask the children to take all the biscuits out of the tin and arrange them on the table. Encourage them to look carefully at the different shapes of the biscuits. Look closely at one of the square-shaped biscuits. How many sides are there? How many corners are there? How many more square-shaped biscuits are there in the tin? What other shapes can they find? Can they name the shapes? How many of each shape are there?

Extension

Ask each child to hold their biscuit in their hand and see if they can find other things in the room which are the same shape as their biscuit. For example, a child who has chosen a round biscuit may notice that the clock is also round.

Talk about

Which biscuits do the children like best? What is it about their favourite biscuit that they like? Have the children noticed other food items that come in different shapes?

Five currant buns

What children should learn

Mathematics – to count with one to one correspondence; to recognize numbers 0 – 5.

What you need

Number symbols 0 – 5 written on large pieces of card; 5 currant buns painted and cut out by the children; 5 pennies.

Activity

Teach the children the action rhyme:

> Five currant buns in a baker's shop,
> Round and fat with a cherry on the top,
> Along came Sally with a penny one day,
> Bought a currant bun and took it right away.

Ask the children to role-play the rhyme as they sing, with one child as the baker, five children, each with a penny, taking it in turns to buy and so on.

Extension

Use the action rhyme 'Ten fat sausages sizzling in a pan, One went pop and another went bang!' to teach counting and number recognition 0 – 10 in the same way. This rhyme is also useful for introducing the concept of subtraction.

Talk about

Have the children ever been shopping in a real bakery and handled money? What was for sale and how were the items displayed and packaged? What did they buy and how much did it cost?

Five currant buns in a baker's shop, Round and fat ...

Oodles of noodles

What children should learn

Personal and social development – to have respect and sensitivity for people of other cultures and enjoy preparing and eating food together.

What you need

An onion; a pepper; cooking oil; 100g mushrooms; a packet of egg noodles; soy sauce; a sharp knife; a wok or large frying pan; a saucepan; paper plates; chopsticks.

Activity

Tell the children that you are going to cook some special Chinese food for everyone in the group to share. Ask the children to wash their hands properly. Finely chop the onion and pepper then fry them in a little oil in the wok, stirring regularly for 2 – 3 minutes. Chop and add the mushrooms. Help the children to cook the noodles in the saucepan, following the instructions on the packet. Drain the noodles, mix with the other ingredients, adding soy sauce to taste. Serve each child a portion on a paper plate. They can eat with their fingers or try to use the chopsticks.

Extension

Make a collection of Chinese artefacts (for example, a lantern, new year's greeting cards, 'ang pow' packets and a chinese dragon) for the children to look at and handle. Share books with photographs about a typical Chinese family. Invite a Chinese person to talk to the children about customs and traditions.

Talk about

Have the children tasted Chinese food before? Do they like it? Discuss how the noodles look, feel and taste. What is it like to eat with chopsticks?

Snack time

What children should learn

Personal and social development – to share and take turns in a group; to develop independence in pouring a drink and in making choices.

What you need

Orange juice and milk in jugs; plastic cups; a selection of fruit cut into bite-sized pieces; a large tray to carry it all on.

Activity

Sit the children around a table. Demonstrate how to pour a drink without spilling it, then pass around the tray with the drinks and cups on, giving each child a turn and praising them for their efforts. Encourage the children to help each other to pass the tray around the circle in between turns. When everyone has finished drinking, choose a child to carry the tray around to collect the cups. Choose a different child to pass around the plate of fruit and to ask everyone, 'What would you like?' Encourage the children to thank each other as they take their piece of fruit.

Extension

Involve the children in the snack preparation. Let them: pour the orange juice and milk from the cartons into the jugs; choose, wash and chop the fruit; and to count the correct number of cups on to the tray.

Talk about

Encourage the children to talk about other things that they are able to do all on their own, both at home and when they come to the group. Talk about other times in the day when they share and take turns. How does it make them feel?

Eggs for Easter

What children should learn

Personal and social development – to learn about and enjoy celebrating the festival of Easter and the growth of new life that springtime brings.

What you need

A copy of the Easter story; eggs, enough for one for each child; fruit and vegetables for colouring the eggs (for example red cabbage for blue dye, beetroot for pink, orange peel to make yellow); vegetable oil and vinegar; saucepans; cooker.

Activity

Tell the children the Easter story and explain that many people celebrate Easter with eggs to represent the dawning of new life. Prepare the fruit or vegetables with the children. These will be needed as colouring for the eggs. Place your eggs and one of the chopped vegetables in a saucepan and cover with cold water. Add a dessertspoon of vinegar, bring to the boil and simmer for 15 – 20 minutes. When the eggs have cooled, help the children rub a little vegetable oil on to the eggshells to make them shine.

Extension

After the eggs have been dyed, they could be decorated further by using either acrylic paints, sequins or shiny sticky pieces of paper. The children could also make Easter cards by decorating cut-out egg shapes with painted patterns, sequins or shiny paper.

Talk about

Do the children know which creatures hatch from eggs? Talk about different life cycles and the ways in which plants, animals and birds begin life. What signs of new life beginning have the children noticed around them?

Kindness cakes

What children should learn

Personal and social development – to gain a sense of pleasure from making a special gift to give to a friend.

What you need

100g self-raising flour; 100g butter or margarine; 100g caster sugar; 100g icing sugar and water to mix; 2 eggs lightly beaten; pinch of salt; sweets or chocolate drops to decorate.

Activity

Ask the children to wash their hands thoroughly and put on their aprons. Help them weigh out the ingredients. Cream the sugar and butter. Add the egg a little at a time, whisking well. Fold in the flour and salt. Place the mixture in cake cases on a baking tray in the oven for 15 – 20 minutes at 375°F/190°C. When the cakes have cooled, the children can decorate them by making smiley faces with the sweets pressed into the icing. While the children are cooking and clearing up, they should be encouraged to think about to whom they might be kind and give their cake as a gift.

Extension

To make their gifts more special, the children could be supported to make and decorate a container to put their cake in. Simple cake containers can be made by decorating circles of card with felt-tipped pen patterns, folding them in half and stapling along the curved edge. These can be filled with brightly coloured shredded paper to help the cakes sit upright inside.

Talk about

How does it make the children feel to receive a gift from a friend? Encourage them to share their experiences with others in the group. How does it make them feel to make and give something special to a friend? What other things have they done, or could they do, to be kind to others?

Brown bear, brown bear, who stole the honey?

What children should learn

Personal and social development – to gain confidence, self-respect and show sensitivity to others.

What you need

A plastic jar of honey.

Activity

Sit the children in a circle on the floor. Select a child to play the brown bear, who curls up 'asleep' in the middle of the circle. Another child places the jar of honey on his back and reminds him 'no peeping'. All the group then chant, 'Isn't it funny how a bear likes honey! Buzz, buzz, buzz, I wonder why he does? Go to sleep Mr Bear!' Another child 'steals' the honey and pretends to hide it, whilst the other children pretend to hide it as well. When this is done, the bear is woken by everyone chanting 'Brown bear, brown bear who's got the honey?' Brown bear then has three chances to guess who has his honey, by asking, 'Have you got my honey?'

Extension

To develop confidence with speaking and listening in a group, the children who are suspected of stealing the honey, but who are innocent, could be asked to give a reason why they did not steal it. For example 'It wasn't me, I don't like honey!' or 'It wasn't me, my mum has just got some honey from the shops!'

Talk about

Where does honey come from? Why do bears like it so much? Read and talk about the story of *Winnie the Pooh*.

Pineapple pictures

What children should learn

Creative development – to explore line, texture, shape and form by making pencil sketches.

What you need

A pineapple; white paper cut into a variety of shapes and sizes; thick-and thin-nibbed pencils; a large sheet of paper; felt-tipped pen to record ideas.

Activity

Sit the children in a small group around a table. Pass the pineapple around and encourage them to look closely at it and touch it. As each child takes their turn to hold the pineapple, ask them to think of words to describe it, guiding their responses by asking questions. Write their ideas down on a large sheet of paper. Re-read the list as a memory jog before they begin their sketches. Ask each child to choose some paper and a pencil and begin to draw what they see. As the children draw, remind them again about all the different things that they saw. Encourage each child to make as many sketches as they wish, choosing different papers and pencils.

Extension

Provide the children with sketchbooks. These could be made from sheets of paper stapled or stitched together, with the cover decorated by each child as they wish. A collection of different fruits and vegetables could then be arranged for the children to sketch. Red cabbage or kiwi fruit cut in half make good subjects.

Talk about

Encourage the children to talk about the shape of the pineapple and its leaves. What shapes and patterns can they see on its surface? Do they notice if some parts of the pineapple look darker than others? How might they show this in their sketches?

Salt dough baking

What children should learn

Creative development – to make representations of real and imaginary foods.

What you need

A bowl and spoon; a rolling pin, knife, fork, pastry cutters; baking trays and an oven; half a cup of salt; one and a half cups of plain flour; water to mix; pictures of pastries, bread and cakes cut from magazines.

Activity

With the children, mix the dry ingredients together, add the water a little at a time and stir well. Use hands to knead the dough and bring it together in a ball. Divide the mixture into smaller balls so that each child has some. Magazine pictures will provide some ideas, but encourage the children to use their imagination. Show them different techniques, such as how to roll the dough into sausages and make spirals, how to roll the dough into small balls and flatten them with the palm of their hand and how to make patterns in the dough with the back of a fork. Place the dough items on the baking trays and put them in a cool oven. They may take several hours to cook depending on the thickness of the dough and will benefit from being turned over once or twice.

Extension

When cool and hard, the dough can be painted and varnished.

Talk about

Discuss the changes that take place from raw ingredients to baked dough. Discuss the way the dough feels, how it can be twisted, stretched or squashed.

The Hungry Giant

What children should learn

Creative development – to respond to a story by making and using a puppet.

What you need

A copy of *The Hungry Giant* (Storychest); paper plates; wooden sticks or strips of strong card about 30cm long; modelling materials: eg, paper plates, bottle tops, wool, string, gummed paper, shiny paper, tissue paper, scraps of fabric; masking tape; glue.

Activity

Read the story of *The Hungry Giant* to the children. Before they begin to work at making their 'giant' puppets, spend some time talking about what sort of character the giant is, encouraging the children to think about what sort of expression he might have on his face. Allow them to select their materials to build up a picture of the giant's face on their paper plate. Talk with them about their choices and how they plan to use the materials. Finally they will need help fixing the wooden stick securely to the plate to make a handle for holding their puppet.

Extension

Working in pairs, the children could use their puppet to pretend to be the hungry giant (they could initially work with an adult but as the children gain confidence they may be able to work with another child). Provide the children with a box of simple props and the book and they will be able to re-enact the story.

Talk about

The story provides a useful starting point for a discussion on kind and unkind behaviour. The children could be encouraged to think of nicer ways in which the giant could ask the people in the story to help him find food.

Hot potato!

What children should learn

Creative development – to explore sound and rhythm by playing a musical game.

What you need

A tambourine.

Activity

Sit the children in a circle. Explain that you are going to pretend that the tambourine is a very hot potato, so hot that you would burn your fingers if you held it for a long time, so it needs to be passed around the circle quickly. As the children pass the tambourine around, encourage them to join in with the rhyme, 'Hot potato, pass it around, hot potato pass it around, hot potato pass it around, get rid of that hot potato!' When the singing stops, whoever is holding the tambourine has a turn to play it, while another child is selected to describe how the tambourine is being played. Allow everyone a turn at finding a new way of playing the tambourine.

Extension

When the singing stops, the child holding the tambourine is encouraged to play a certain number of beats. Another child then has to count and say how many beats were played.

Talk about

Describe different ways of playing the tambourine. Describe the different qualities of sound that you can make. How does it make you feel when you play the tambourine quickly, slowly, loudly or quietly?

The Enormous Turnip

What children should learn

Physical development – to move imaginatively with increasing control and co-ordination.

What you need

A copy of the traditional story *The Enormous Turnip* (in the anthology *Just Like Me*, Storychest).

Activity

Read *The Enormous Turnip* to the children and show the children the pictures. In small groups, act out the story: weeding the ground, raking the soil, digging a hole, opening the seed packet, planting and watering the seed. Make the sun shine and the rain pour and show with your hands how every day the turnip is growing bigger and bigger and bigger. When it is time to harvest the turnip, act out all the different characters that come to help pull it up. Finally, act out washing, peeling, chopping, cooking and eating the turnip.

Extension

With the children, plant some real vegetable seeds in your own vegetable patch or maybe a growbag. Turnips probably will not be as appealing as pumpkins. These seeds, if watered regularly, grow well, reaching an impressive size. Runner beans and tomatoes also grow fairly rapidly and are easy to look after.

Talk about

Has anyone tasted turnip before and what did they think of it? Have they planted seeds at home or helped to prepare vegetables in the kitchen? Try to recall the sequence of events in the story. Make a list of all that had to be done to grow, harvest and cook the turnip.

Making pizza

What children should learn

Physical development – to use a range of kitchen utensils with increasing control and co-ordination.

What you need

100g self-raising flour; pinch of salt; 25g margarine; 2 tablespoons milk and 2 tablespoons water; 50g hard cheese; half an onion, finely chopped; 3 tomatoes, sliced; 3 mushrooms, sliced; tomato puree; 1 teaspoon dried mixed herbs; salt and pepper; large mixing bowl; several small bowls; a sieve; a rolling pin; a baking tray; a grater; a sharp knife; a chopping board; a tablespoon and a teaspoon; an oven set at 425°F (220°C).

Activity

Support the children with washing their hands thoroughly before the food preparation begins. Help them sieve the flour, add salt and rub in the margarine. Gradually add in the milk and water. Mix the ingredients together to make a soft dough. Help the children to grate the cheese, chop the onion and slice the tomatoes and mushrooms, placing each ingredient into one of the smaller bowls. Now they can roll out the dough to about 1cm thick and place it on the baking tray. Finally they can spread a little tomato puree over the base, put on the tomatoes, onions and mushrooms, sprinkle the grated cheese on top and season the pizza with herbs, salt and pepper. Cook for 15 – 20 minutes.

Extension

How many children in the group would like to taste the pizza? How can they make sure the pizza is shared fairly between everyone who wants a piece?

Talk about

Have the children tasted pizza before? Where did they taste it, at home or at a pizza place? Which toppings do they like best on their pizza? Do they ever help to cook or do other jobs at home?

Jumping beans

What children should learn

Physical development – to co-ordinate body movements with increasing control and develop an awareness of moving safely in a large space with other people.

What you need

A large empty space; a tambourine.

Activity

With the children, practise walking/moving around the room or playground in your own space and not bumping into anyone. Introduce the tambourine: when they hear it, they must all stop, stand still and listen for instructions. To encourage a variety of movement, you could call out 'Jumping beans' and tell the children to jump up and down from space to space. If you were to call 'Runner beans' – the children would start running about avoiding any collisions; 'Broad beans' – stand still being as wide as possible; 'Jelly beans' – stand, shake and wobble their bodies; 'Beanstalk' – stand on tiptoes stretched up tall, hands above their heads.

Extension

Can the children move in time to the beat of the tambourine? Play different beats to accompany the different movements, for example a slow rhythm for jumping, a faster rhythm for running, two beats only for broad beans, a long shake for jelly beans and a very loud beat for beanstalk! Can the children adapt to the changing rhythms instead of your instructions?

Talk about

Make a collection of different sorts of beans and discuss the similarities and differences between them. Which sorts of beans do the children like to eat best? Do a survey in your group to find out which are the most popular.

A healthy lunchbox

What children should learn

Knowledge and understanding of the world – to sort foods into groups according to whether they are healthy or not healthy.

What you need

A lunchbox; a selection of foods, for example an apple, a chocolate bar, a packet of crisps, a yoghurt, a cheese sandwich, a jam sandwich, carrot sticks, biscuits, cakes, a carton of orange juice, a fizzy drink.

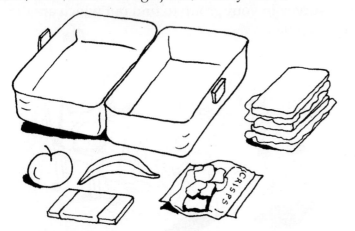

Activity

Without showing the children the food or the lunchbox, ask them what they think the word 'healthy' means. Talk about the things that help us to stay healthy, and what happens to our bodies when we feel ill. Ask the children to look at each of the food items in turn and discuss whether they help us to stay healthy or not. Encourage the children to give reasons for their choices. All of the 'healthy' foods can then be placed inside the lunchbox.

Extension

Sorting empty packets, cartons, tins and pots brought from home, the children could set up a healthy food shop. Using pictures of food cut from magazines, they could make posters of healthy food to display in their shop.

Talk about

What did the children have for their breakfast or lunch? Was it healthy? Share the story of *The Very Hungry Caterpillar* by Eric Carle and discuss which of the foods that the caterpillar eats are healthy.

Investigating jelly

What children should learn

Knowledge and understanding of the world – to develop the ability to observe closely and describe changes.

What you need

A packet of jelly; a kettle; a transparent mixing bowl; a wooden spoon; children's scissors; a measuring jug; a fridge.

Activity

Help the children to separate the jelly into cubes, talking about what they see, feel and smell. Follow the instructions on the packet. Ask the children to stir the mixture and watch closely to see if they notice any changes. When the jelly has dissolved, the children can measure in the cold water, again watching to see if they notice any changes. Help the children to put the jelly in the fridge and leave it overnight. The following day look at the jelly again and talk about what has happened. Help the children to spoon the jelly into plastic cups. Now you can enjoy eating it!

Extension

Make a collage to display on the wall. Use different papers to represent the various states of the jelly. Take photographs of the children investigating the jelly to add to the display. Write their comments on large cut-out speech bubbles and add these too.

Talk about

Can the children identify the flavour of the jelly just by smelling it? Talk about the changing states (solid – liquid – solid). Discuss what made these changes happen. What else changes state when added to water, heated up or cooled down?

What's in the box?

What children should learn

Knowledge and understanding of the world – to learn to differentiate between a variety of foods using the senses of smell and touch.

What you need

Small quantities of food stuffs with a distinctive smell and texture, for example onion, cheese, chocolate, orange, honey, strawberries, fresh bread, cucumber; washed-out yoghurt pots; muslin or thin cotton; elastic bands; a cardboard box; scissors.

Activity

Cut a hole in the box opposite the opening, large enough for a child's hand. Place a food item inside each yoghurt pot and cover with the muslin secured by the elastic band. Explain to the children that each one will take a turn to guess what it is, by smelling or touching but not looking. After they have smelt the item in the yoghurt pot, place it in the cardboard box, taking off the muslin. Let the children put their hands through the holes in the box and feel the item. After they have made their guess, show them whether they are right or wrong.

Extension

Make a simple grid for the children to record with a tick or a cross whether or not they were able to identify each food. They can then count to see how many they got right and how many they got wrong, and compare their responses with their friends'.

Talk about

Encourage the children to work together in a group to think of as many words as they can to describe each food item. These words can then be listed and made into a poem.

Sprouting beans

What children should learn

Knowledge and understanding of the world – to observe the changes in seeds as they grow.

What you need

Mung beans; a tablespoon; a large plastic jar; cold water; muslin and an elastic band to cover the top of the jar; a warm, dark place.

Activity

Explain to the children that they are going to grow some bean sprouts which they can eat. Help them to count out four tablespoons of beans, place them in the jar and cover them with cold water. Secure the muslin firmly on top of the jar. Find a warm, dark place for the beans to grow. The beans can be left to soak overnight then any excess water poured out. The beans will need rinsing in clean water two or three times a day (this can be done without removing the muslin). The beans should be ready to eat in three to four days.

Extension

Encourage the children to think about the conditions needed for the beans to grow: hot, cold, light or dark. Some jars of beans could be prepared and grown in different conditions to find out how they grow best.

Talk about

What changes do the children notice as the beans begin to sprout? Use a magnifying glass to see more clearly. Together, think of words that describe the shape, size, colour, texture and taste of the sprouting beans. Discuss ways in which the bean sprouts could be prepared to be eaten.

Picnic basket

What children should learn

Knowledge and understanding of the world – to use cutting, folding and joining skills to make a picnic basket for a cuddly toy.

What you need

A selection of cardboard boxes, for example cereal packets, teabag boxes, frozen food cartons; glue, sticky tape, masking tape, split pins; a selection of used wrapping papers; strips of flexible card for handles; scissors.

Activity

Discuss various designs of baskets before beginning to make one. You will need to discuss: what type of handle? Will it need a lid? How big will it be? Provide some real picnic baskets or pictures for the children to look at (this will help them make their decisions). Once they have selected the materials they will use, help them decide where to start and which method of joining would be appropriate. When the picnic basket is made, the wrapping paper can be used to either line or completely cover it.

Extension

Plan a cuddly toys' picnic together with the children. What would they like to eat? What does their cuddly toy like to eat? What games would they like to play? The children could make jam or honey sandwiches, biscuits and cakes to put in their baskets.

Talk about

In a small group, encourage each child to talk about how they made their basket, which materials they chose and how they joined them together. Compare and contrast the different designs to share ideas and show the children that there is more than one way of solving a problem.